KEEP YOUR COOL:
ANGER MANAGEMENT JOURNAL FOR KIDS

ANGER MANAGEMENT
Journal for kids

Explore Your Feelings, Find Calm, and Express Yourself

Hiedi France, EdD

ROCKRIDGE
PRESS

This book is dedicated to my husband. You grew up with so much anger. Your circumstances presented many situations that warranted it. You are an inspiration for anyone who struggles with anger. You found your way. I love you immensely!

Contents

Introduction

I am so glad you are here! This book is all about you. It is a user guide to help you understand the most important person: *you*! I like to think of this book as a hack for better living. There is something magical about this book. We are going to use your ideas and thoughts to help you understand this thing called anger. We all feel angry sometimes. We all struggle with anger sometimes. This is okay! I want you to repeat this to yourself: Anger is okay, and we all struggle sometimes.

This journal has three parts. The first part will be exploring how you feel. Learning about different feelings helps us know when they are happening. The second part is about calming uncomfortable feelings. We all have emotions that don't make us feel good, but this book can help you learn how to feel better. The third part of the book is about doing things that help us get our needs met. Uncomfortable feelings come when we want or need something. This can be hard. You will learn there are things you can do to feel better.

This book has more than 100 different prompts. Each prompt begins with a check-in. You will identify how you are feeling right now and why. The more you do this, the better you will be at recognizing how your feelings change over time. This is okay. Remember, all feelings are okay. Once you check in, you will do either a writing, drawing, or doing activity. These are to help you manage your feelings and express yourself. Be honest about how you see things. This book is all about you!

This is your book. Write in it. Draw in it. Make lots of doodles. There is no right way to use this book. You can go in order or jump around. There may be some activities you want to skip. Do it! Just come back to them later.

How you are feeling might change and you might want to complete the activities you skipped.

Are you ready to get started? I believe in you. I know you can do this!

PART 1

EXPLORING MY FEELINGS

What are feelings? Feelings are sensations we have when something happens. They are our body or brain's reactions to things around us. These reactions help us survive. All feelings are okay, even the hard ones like sadness or anger. In this section, we will learn about many different feelings.

MY FEELINGS

How am I feeling right now?

I feel this way because __I AM CALM__

___

We all have feelings. Think about some feelings you have had in the last week. Write as many as you can think of.

_____   _____

_____   _____

_____   _____

_____   _____

_____   _____

_____   _____

_____   _____

 Look over your list. Circle the feelings that you felt the strongest.

FEELINGS I LIKE

How am I feeling right now?

I feel this way because _____

_____

Comfortable feelings are ones we like. We want to experience more of them. Name a feeling that's comfortable for you.

_____

What happens to make you feel this way?

_____

_____

_____

_____

_____

How can you help yourself feel this way more often?

_____

_____

_____

FEELINGS I DON'T LIKE

How am I feeling right now?

I feel this way because _____

_____

Uncomfortable feelings are ones we do not like. We often try to avoid these feelings. Name a feeling that is uncomfortable for you.

_____

What happens to make you feel this way?

_____

_____

_____

_____

How can you help yourself feel better?

_____

_____

_____

_____

PICTURE IT!

How am I feeling right now?

I feel this way because _____

_____

Feelings can also make us think of things around us. For example, someone might imagine a flower or the sun when they think about being happy. Pick a feeling and draw what you think of when you think of that feeling.

RAINBOW OF FEELINGS

How am I feeling right now?

I feel this way because _____

_____

We can also think about feelings in colors. Everyone can think of feelings in different colors.

*My **blue** feelings are:*

_____

_____

*My **yellow** feelings are:*

_____

_____

*My **red** feelings are:*

_____

_____

*My **green** feelings are:*

_____

_____

My _____ *feelings are:*

_____

_____

_____

BEHIND THE FEELING

How am I feeling right now?

I feel this way because _____

_____

Things around us can make us feel different ways. Think of three things. What does each thing make you feel? Why do you think that is?

_____

_____

_____

_____

_____

_____

_____

_____

_____

_____

_____

WORD FINDER

How am I feeling right now?

I feel this way because _____

_____

It is helpful to be able to use our words to tell others how we feel. Think of three feelings you had this week. What made you have those feelings? Write how you felt and why.

I felt _____ when _____

_____ happened,

because _____

_____ .

I felt _____ when _____

_____ happened,

because _____

_____ .

I felt _____ when _____

_____ happened,

because _____

_____ .

FACIAL CLUES

How am I feeling right now?

I feel this way because _____

_____

Sometimes we can tell how someone is feeling by looking at their face. A sad face might have a frown. A happy face might have a smile. These are facial clues. Practice reading these clues in this activity.

1. Find a mirror.

2. Think of a feeling.

3. Look at your face.

4. Notice how your eyes, eyebrows, and mouth look.

Write about how your face looked for two different feelings.

Feeling: _____

_____

_____

Feeling: _____

_____

_____

How am I feeling right now?

I feel this way because _____

_____

We can also look at body clues to know how someone feels. When you are happy, your arms might feel light and your feet might be still.

1. Find a quiet spot.

2. Think about feeling sad.

3. What do your head, arms, and feet feel like?

4. Now think about other feelings, like happy, mad, or scared.

Pick one feeling. How did your body feel? What were the clues?

Feeling: _____

Head:

_____

_____

_____

_____

_____

Arms:

Feet:

UNDERSTANDING ANGER

How am I feeling right now?

I feel this way because _____

_____

Knowing our anger helps us understand it. Remember, anger is okay to feel. We can learn more about it, and when we understand our anger, it is less scary.

How often do you feel angry?

_____

_____

What makes you feel angry?

_____

_____

_____

What do you do when you are angry?

_____

_____

_____

MY ANGER

How am I feeling right now?

I feel this way because _____

_____

Anger can be an unexpected feeling. It is best when we can think about what causes us to be angry. Think about the last time you felt angry. Draw what happened.

SADNESS

How am I feeling right now?

I feel this way because _____

_____

Anger can be caused by other feelings, too. Sadness is when something unhappy happens. Think of a time when you have been sad.

What did it feel like?

_____

_____

_____

_____

_____

How did you handle it?

_____

_____

_____

_____

_____

DISAPPOINTMENT

How am I feeling right now?

I feel this way because _____

_____

Disappointment can sometimes feel like anger. Disappointment is a feeling that might happen when we don't get what we want. Think of a time when you have been disappointed.

What did it feel like?

_____

_____

_____

_____

_____

How did you handle it?

_____

_____

_____

_____

_____

How am I feeling right now?

I feel this way because _____

_____

Another sensation that can feel like anger is jealousy. Jealousy is when we want something that someone else has. Think of a time when you have been jealous.

What did it feel like?

_____

_____

_____

_____

How did you handle it?

_____

_____

_____

_____

_____

EMBARRASSMENT

How am I feeling right now?

I feel this way because _____

_____

When we feel embarrassed, we might also feel anger. We feel embarrassed when something happens that we are ashamed about. Think of a time when you have felt embarrassed.

What did it feel like?

_____

_____

_____

_____

How did you handle it?

_____

_____

_____

_____

_____

How am I feeling right now?

I feel this way because _____

_____

Worry can also make us feel anger. This happens when we are concerned about something or someone. Think of a time when you have been worried.

What did it feel like?

_____

_____

_____

_____

How did you handle it?

_____

_____

_____

_____

_____

How am I feeling right now?

I feel this way because _____

_____

Anger can overwhelm our whole body and brain, but we can learn to pause our anger. Try following these steps.

1. Pause what you are doing.

2. Take three deep breaths.

3. Focus on something you like.

4. Keep doing this until you feel better.

Think about the last time you were angry. How would pausing have helped you?

_____

_____

_____

_____

_____

_____

_____

A PORTRAIT OF ANGER

How am I feeling right now?

I feel this way because _____

_____

Anger can be a big emotion. Draw your anger. Use colors and shapes to help show what anger looks like to you.

ANGER LEVELS

How am I feeling right now?

I feel this way because _____

_____

Not all anger feels the same. There are different levels of anger. Sometimes we feel a little bit of anger. Other times we are very angry. Remember all levels of anger are okay. We just need to learn how to handle them.

I feel a little bit of anger when _____

_____

I feel some anger when _____

_____

I feel a lot of anger when _____

_____

I feel the most anger when _____

_____

How am I feeling right now?

I feel this way because _____

_____

Everyone feels grumpy sometimes. Feeling grumpy means that we might be tired or easily upset. Write about what it feels like when you are grumpy.

_____

_____

_____

_____

_____

What helps you when you feel grumpy?

_____

_____

_____

_____

_____

IRRITATED

How am I feeling right now?

I feel this way because _____

_____

We all also feel irritated sometimes. Feeling irritated is when everything seems to be bothering us. Write about a time when you felt irritated.

_____

_____

_____

_____

_____

What helps you when you feel irritated?

_____

_____

_____

_____

_____

FRUSTRATED

How am I feeling right now?

I feel this way because _____

_____

We can feel frustrated when something is hard or unexpected.
Write about a time when you felt frustrated.

_____

_____

_____

_____

_____

What helps you when you feel frustrated?

_____

_____

_____

_____

_____

_____

FURIOUS

How am I feeling right now?

I feel this way because _____

_____

We feel furious when our body is full of anger. It is hard to keep our cool. Write about a time when you felt furious.

_____

_____

_____

_____

_____

What helps you when you feel furious?

_____

_____

_____

_____

_____

_____

How am I feeling right now?

I feel this way because _____

_____

Rage is a feeling when we lose all control of our anger. It comes pouring out and is very hard to stop. Write about a time when you felt rage.

_____

_____

_____

_____

_____

What helps you when you feel rage?

_____

_____

_____

_____

_____

_____

ANGER VOLCANO

How am I feeling right now?

I feel this way because _____

_____

A big feeling like anger can be like a volcano. Our feelings can go from calm to furious very quickly. Understanding what makes us feel different levels of anger can help us. Draw things that make you feel types of anger below.

How am I feeling right now?

I feel this way because _____

_____

Sometimes we can simply breathe away our anger. When you feel anger come over you, try following these steps to let it go.

1. Put your feet on the ground.

2. Think about three things that make you happy.

3. Take three deep breaths.

4. Breathe in your happy things and breathe out the anger.

How did that feel? Write three words to describe how you felt after this exercise.

_____

_____

_____

_____

_____

_____

_____

UPSETTING THINGS

How am I feeling right now?

I feel this way because _____

_____

We can feel upset for many reasons. Draw things that make you upset on the left and things that make you feel better on the right.

How am I feeling right now?

I feel this way because _____

_____

Anger can help tell us that something is wrong inside. Our body gives clues about how we are feeling. Think about the last time you were hungry, tired, bored, sick, or lonely.

How did your head feel?

_____

_____

_____

_____

_____

_____

_____

_____

_____

_____

_____

How did your stomach feel?

_____

_____

_____

_____

_____

_____

_____

_____

What else did you notice about how your body felt?

_____

_____

_____

_____

_____

_____

_____

_____

THOUGHT CONTROL

How am I feeling right now?

I feel this way because _____

_____

What we think about can make our anger smaller or bigger. We can control our thoughts, which means we can think of things that can make us feel better.

What thoughts make your anger bigger?

_____

_____

_____

_____

_____

What thoughts make your anger smaller?

_____

_____

_____

_____

HAPPY THINGS

How am I feeling right now?

I feel this way because _____

_____

We can all find ways to keep our anger under control. Thinking about things that make us happy can help. Draw yourself doing something that makes you happy.

SLEEP TIGHT

How am I feeling right now?

I feel this way because _____

_____

Being tired can make our anger harder to control. Getting a good night's sleep is a great way to ease our anger. Having a bedtime routine can help. Try this routine if you are having a hard time falling asleep.

1. Turn off all lights and electronics.

2. Lie down.

3. Focus on your breathing.

4. Clear your mind or think happy thoughts.

How did you like that? What would you change?

_____

_____

_____

_____

_____

_____

_____

HUNGER

How am I feeling right now?

I feel this way because _____

_____

Being hungry can make us feel grumpy. Eating healthy food can help keep us full longer. Eating on a regular schedule can also help.

What foods do you like to eat?
List them below.

_____ _____

_____ _____

_____ _____

_____ _____

_____ _____

_____ _____

Circle the foods that you think are the healthiest.

OUTSIDE TRIGGERS

How am I feeling right now?

I feel this way because _____

_____

Triggers for anger can also come from things around us. We are not always in control of these things. If we identify the things around us that cause anger, we are better able to handle the anger because we can be prepared.

Which people upset you most?

_____

_____

What things upset you most?

_____

_____

What activities upset you most?

_____

_____

PEOPLE

How am I feeling right now?

I feel this way because _____

_____

There are some people we can feel more upset around. This can be because we spend a lot of time with them, so we get to know them better than most. Think about someone who upsets you a lot.

Why do you think they are so upsetting?

_____

_____

_____

_____

_____

What would help make it better?

_____

_____

_____

_____

How am I feeling right now?

I feel this way because _____

_____

Our anger can be triggered by things that are upsetting. For example, certain clothes or other items can cause much frustration. Think about something that upsets you a lot.

Why do you think that thing is so upsetting?

_____

_____

_____

_____

_____

What would help make it better?

_____

_____

_____

_____

How am I feeling right now?

I feel this way because _____

_____

Certain activities, like games or schoolwork, can be upsetting. We can feel frustrated if we lose a game or have trouble understanding something. Think about an activity that upsets you a lot.

Why do you think that activity is so upsetting?

_____

_____

_____

_____

_____

What would help make it better?

_____

_____

_____

_____

WALK IT OFF

How am I feeling right now?

I feel this way because _____

_____

Some things that upset us are not in our control, but we can learn to walk away from them. Try this the next time a person, thing, or activity is upsetting.

1. Pause your body and brain.

2. Ask to leave the area.

3. Go somewhere quiet or relaxing.

4. Think about your happy things.

Did walking away help you keep your cool?

_____

_____

_____

_____

_____

_____

_____

PART 2

FINDING CALM

Anger is never forever. It comes, but it also leaves. We can find ways to feel better when we are angry. This section will help you explore ways to breathe, move, think of something else, and use support. Remember, anger is okay. We just need to learn how to handle it.

CALMING THINGS

How am I feeling right now?

I feel this way because _____

_____

No one likes being angry. We try hard to feel better. We can do this by thinking about things that calm us, like a favorite person or blanket. Draw some things that make you feel better when you are upset.

DEEP BREATHS

How am I feeling right now?

I feel this way because _____

_____

Deep breaths can help us calm down. You can do this by breathing in through your nose slowly and then breathing out through your mouth. Practice by following these steps.

1. Breathe in through your nose.

2. Breathe out through your mouth.

3. Repeat two more times.

How did that feel?

_____

_____

_____

_____

Did you like this breathing exercise?

TAKE A BREATH

How am I feeling right now?

I feel this way because _____

_____

Using our breath is one way we can calm ourselves. Taking a slow or deep breath can help your body and brain calm down. Take a few deep breaths and write about how it makes you feel.

My head feels: _____

_____

My arms feel: _____

_____

My legs feel: _____

_____

My stomach feels: _____

_____

My _____ *feels:* _____

_____

_____

ANIMAL BREATHING

I feel this way because _____

_____

Animals breathe, too. We can take deep breaths like an animal. Can you pant like a dog or maybe take a big, deep breath like a whale? Write down as many animals as you can think of.

_____ _____

_____ _____

_____ _____

Look over your list. Breathe like you are one of the animals you listed.

How did that feel?

_____

_____

_____

Did you like this breathing exercise?

IMAGINATION BREATHING

I feel this way because _____

_____

We can use our imagination while breathing. We can visualize ourselves in different places. Write down a place that makes you feel happy. For example, you could write down the beach, the playground, or some other place you like.

_____

_____

_____

Close your eyes and imagine you are there. Take five deep breaths.

How did that feel?

_____

_____

_____

Did you like this breathing exercise?

How am I feeling right now?

I feel this way because _____

_____

Counting as we breathe also helps us calm down. Write the numbers 1 to 10 below.

_____

_____

_____

_____

Count from 1 to 10 while slowly breathing in and out.

How did that feel?

_____

_____

_____

_____

Did you like this breathing exercise?

BREATHE AND HOLD

I feel this way because _____

_____

We can learn to hold our breath for a short time. This helps give our brain time to rest. Try the below steps and see if you like it.

1. Breathe in through your nose.

2. Hold your breath.

3. Count to three.

4. Breathe out through your mouth.

How did that feel?

_____

_____

_____

_____

_____

Did you like this breathing exercise?

SHAPE BREATHING

I feel this way because _____

_____

You can use shapes to breathe and hold. Write down as many shapes as you can.

_____

_____

_____

Look over your list. Try to think how you can breathe and hold for each shape. For example, you can breathe in for each side and breathe out at each corner.

How did that feel?

_____

_____

_____

Did you like this breathing exercise?

SUCCESS STORY

How am I feeling right now?

I feel this way because _____

_____

Taking deep breaths can be hard when we are upset. Write about a time when you were able to calm down by taking deep breaths.

_____

_____

_____

_____

_____

How did it make you feel?

_____

_____

_____

_____

_____

_____

MY BODY IN MOTION

How am I feeling right now?

I feel this way because _____

_____

Think about the last time you used movement to help calm yourself. Maybe you went for a walk or ran in place. Draw what happened.

MOVE YOUR BODY

How am I feeling right now?

I feel this way because _____

_____

Moving our bodies can be a great way to calm down. It helps our brain cool down, too. There are many ways we can move when upset. Knowing which types of movements you like can help you calm down.

What ways do you like to move your body?

_____

_____

_____

_____

_____

_____

_____

_____

_____

_____

_____

What ways do you not like to move your body?

_____

_____

_____

_____

_____

_____

_____

_____

How does movement help you calm down?

_____

_____

_____

_____

_____

_____

_____

_____

YOGA

I feel this way because _____

_____

Yoga is a way to move our bodies while breathing deeply. It can be done alone or with other people.

Write about a time when you practiced yoga as a way to calm down.

_____

_____

How did it feel?

_____

_____

Did it help you feel calm? Why or why not?

_____

_____

How am I feeling right now?

I feel this way because _____

_____

Exercise that takes a lot of energy, like running or dancing, helps make your body healthy. It also can help clear your mind.

Write about the last time you exercised.

_____

_____

How did it feel?

_____

_____

Did it help you calm down? Why or why not?

_____

_____

_____

WALKING

I feel this way because _____

_____

Walking is another form of exercise that can calm our bodies.

Write about a time you went for a walk.

_____

_____

_____

How did it feel?

_____

_____

_____

_____

Did it help you calm down?

STRETCHING

How am I feeling right now?

I feel this way because _____

_____

Stretching our bodies can release tension in our muscles. We can do this with both small and large muscles, and we can hold the stretch for a long time or a short time.

Write about the last time you stretched your body.

_____

_____

_____

How did it feel?

_____

_____

_____

Did it help you feel better?

SPORTS

I feel this way because _____

_____

Participating in a sport or game requires us to move with purpose. This means moving our bodies to achieve a goal. This can be scoring a point or having fun.

Write about the last time you played a sport or game.

_____

_____

_____

How did it feel?

_____

_____

_____

Did it help you feel better?

How am I feeling right now?

I feel this way because _____

_____

When we move more of our muscles, we can calm ourselves down faster. Think about how you can move your body using as many muscles as possible. Draw yourself doing the movement.

ONE STEP AT A TIME

How am I feeling right now?

I feel this way because _____

_____

Movement with a plan is better than confused movement. We can sequence movement so that our brains and bodies get calm at the same time. Give it a try. Do movement in this sequence.

1. Pause: Close your eyes and take three deep breaths.

2. Fast: Move your body quickly until you are out of breath.

3. Slow: Move your body slowly until you catch your breath.

Repeat steps 1 to 3 until you are calm. Each time, change how you move your body. For example, you can run during one sequence and dance during the next.

How did it feel?

_____

_____

_____

Did it help you feel better?

THINGS I ENJOY

I feel this way because _____

_____

Anger can keep us from doing the things we like. Often, when we are angry we don't enjoy pleasant things. Think about all the things you do enjoy. Draw a few of them here.

BREAK TIME

How am I feeling right now?

I feel this way because _____

_____

When we are upset, it can be helpful not to think about it, but to do or think of something else instead. This anger break can help you feel better. Then you can go back and deal with what is upsetting you.

I could take an anger break the next time

_____

_____

_____

_____

_____

_____

_____

_____

_____

_____

On my anger break, I could

_____

_____

_____

_____

_____

_____

_____

I would know I feel better when

_____

_____

_____

_____

_____

_____

_____

_____

_____

A GOOD BEAT

How am I feeling right now?

I feel this way because _____

_____

Music can be a great break from anger. It can help us think about other things.

What music do you like?

_____

_____

_____

How do you feel when you listen to music?

_____

_____

_____

Do you think listening to music could help you deal with anger?

How am I feeling right now?

I feel this way because _____

_____

Reading a book or magazine can help when we're upset. It lets our minds focus on the character or story.

What do you like to read?

_____

_____

_____

How do you feel when you read?

_____

_____

_____

Do you think reading a book could help you deal with anger?

How am I feeling right now?

I feel this way because _____

_____

Playing a game or doing a puzzle can be good exercise for our brains. Our brains can focus on that rather than what is upsetting us.

What games do you like to play?

_____

_____

_____

How do you feel when you play games?

_____

_____

_____

Do you think playing a game could help you deal with anger?

How am I feeling right now?

I feel this way because _____

_____

Watching television can help us focus on something else other than our anger. Our favorite shows can be a good anger break.

What shows do you like to watch?

_____

_____

_____

How do you feel when you watch TV?

_____

_____

_____

Do you think watching television could help you deal with anger?

How am I feeling right now?

I feel this way because _____

_____

Anger can be exhausting. Taking a nap or sleeping it off can help us think more clearly.

Where do you like to nap?

_____

_____

_____

How do you feel when you nap?

_____

_____

_____

Do you think taking a nap could help you deal with anger?

ANGER VACATION

How am I feeling right now?

I feel this way because _____

_____

Taking an anger break can be like a vacation. Imagine yourself doing one of the anger break activities: listening to music, reading, playing games, watching TV, napping, or anything else you enjoy. Draw what you are doing and thinking instead of being angry.

FLY AWAY

I feel this way because _____

_____

Anger is not something that stays with us forever. It eventually goes away. Visualize it going away by doing this activity.

1. Get a lightweight item, like a feather, leaf, or flower petal.

2. Visualize that item as your anger.

3. Hold the item flat on your palm.

4. Blow the item as far from your hand as possible.

5. Let all the anger go and start fresh.

How did that feel? Write three words to describe how you felt after this exercise.

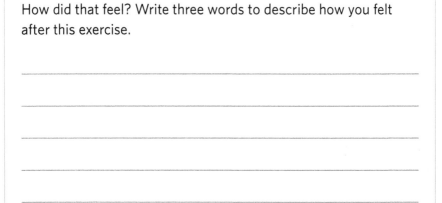

MY BUDDIES

How am I feeling right now?

I feel this way because _____

_____

Having people around us when we are upset can help. Draw some people who comfort you when you are upset.

SUPPORT SYSTEM

How am I feeling right now?

I feel this way because _____

_____

When we are upset, certain people—like a parent or a friend—can help us feel better. They can help support us until the anger is better.

Who do you go to when you are upset?

_____

_____

_____

_____

_____

_____

_____

_____

_____

_____

_____

What does this person do that helps you?

_____

_____

_____

_____

_____

_____

_____

_____

How does this person make you feel?

_____

_____

_____

_____

_____

_____

_____

_____

How am I feeling right now?

I feel this way because _____

_____

Physical contact can help us calm down. Getting a hug from someone can help us better handle anger.

Who would you go to for a hug?

_____

_____

_____

How do hugs make you feel?

_____

_____

_____

Do you think a hug could help you deal with anger?

TALK IT OVER

How am I feeling right now?

I feel this way because _____

_____

Talking can help us calm down. Having someone to talk to when we're upset is important. We can also talk to ourselves through journaling.

Who do you talk to when you are upset?

_____

_____

_____

How does talking make you feel?

_____

_____

_____

Do you think talking or journaling could help you deal with anger?

LET IT OUT

I feel this way because _____

_____

Talking things through can really help, but sometimes we don't have someone to talk to. Still, we can always talk to ourselves. We can also talk through things we may not want to share with someone else this way. Try this activity the next time you are angry.

1. Go to a place where you can be alone.

2. Talk out loud to yourself.

3. Don't filter your thoughts or feelings.

4. Do this until you feel better.

How did you like that? What would you change?

_____

_____

_____

_____

_____

_____

How am I feeling right now?

I feel this way because _____

_____

Softness helps our body and brain calm down. The soft touch of a blanket or a stuffed bear can really make a difference.

What soft items do you like when you are upset?

_____

_____

_____

How does the softness help you?

_____

_____

_____

Do you think something soft could help you deal with anger?

SUPPORT ITEMS

How am I feeling right now?

I feel this way because _____

_____

Things we have can help us when we are upset. These things help us feel calm or happy. Using these items can help us better handle anger.

What item do you like when you are upset?

_____

_____

_____

_____

_____

_____

_____

_____

_____

_____

_____

How does this item help you?

_____

_____

_____

_____

_____

_____

_____

How does this item make you feel?

_____

_____

_____

_____

_____

_____

_____

FAVORITE TOY

I feel this way because _____

_____

Our favorite toys bring comfort. This is true even if you don't play with toys anymore. A toy from the past can bring happy memories.

What is your favorite toy?

_____

_____

_____

How does that toy make you feel?

_____

_____

_____

Do you think playing with that toy could help you deal with anger?

How am I feeling right now?

I feel this way because _____

_____

Pets can be calming. They let us hug them and care for them. If we don't have a pet, we can watch the birds from our windows or spend time with a friend or family member's pet.

What type of pet do you have or want?

_____

_____

_____

How does the pet help you feel better?

_____

_____

_____

Do you think caring for a pet could help you deal with anger?

COMFORT SPOT

I feel this way because _____

_____

It is good to have a place to go when we're upset. This could be a quiet place at home or outside. Take time to create a comfort spot so it is ready when you need it.

1. Find a place that is quiet or relaxing.

2. Gather one or two comfort items.

3. Place the items in the space.

4. Use your comfort spot when you need to calm down.

How did creating a comfort spot make you feel?

_____

_____

_____

_____

_____

_____

PART 3

EXPRESSING MYSELF

We have talked about what anger is and how to calm it. The next step is to find ways to express your emotions in healthy ways. After you have calmed you can think about why you felt angry. This is important because you can try to do something different next time. This section will help you explore healthier ways to express yourself.

MANAGING ANGER

How am I feeling right now?

I feel this way because _____

_____

How we think or talk about anger can make the anger feel bigger or smaller. We can think about anger as something we can deal with or something that overwhelms us. When we are able to have positive thoughts or words about anger, we can better deal with it. Fill in these statements with positive thoughts or words.

I think anger is _____

_____

_____

_____

_____

_____

_____

_____

_____

_____

When anger comes, I can deal with it by _____

_____

_____

_____

_____

_____

One way anger has helped me is _____

_____

_____

_____

_____

_____

I can use anger to _____

_____

_____

_____

_____

_____

USING MY WORDS

How am I feeling right now?

I feel this way because _____

_____

We can use our words to tell other people how we feel. This helps them understand why we are upset. The first step is to identify how we are feeling.

Write as many words as you can think of that describe feeling angry.

_____

_____

_____

_____

Use the words you thought of to fill in these sentences:

I feel _____ when _____ .

I feel _____ when _____ .

I feel _____ when _____ .

How am I feeling right now?

I feel this way because _____

_____

We can also tell others what we need when we are upset. Think about the last time you were upset. What did you need to feel better?

_____

_____

When I am upset, I need _____

_____

_____

_____

When I get my needs met, I feel _____

_____

_____

_____

How am I feeling right now?

I feel this way because _____

_____

When we have to think or talk about anger, it can make us more upset. We can practice how to tell others when we are upset. Practice by following these steps.

1. Go to a quiet place with a mirror.

2. Think about a time when you were upset.

3. Looking at yourself in the mirror, tell yourself how you were feeling.

How did that feel?

_____

_____

_____

_____

Did you like this exercise?

How am I feeling right now?

I feel this way because _____

_____

We can tell others what we feel and need. This can help our anger get smaller. Think about a time when you were upset. Use what you learned on pages 90–92 to put together how you felt and what you needed.

I felt _____

_____

I needed _____

_____

Think about another time you were upset.

I felt _____

_____

I needed _____

_____

How am I feeling right now?

I feel this way because _____

_____

We all have a little voice inside our head. It can help us either calm down or stay angry. We can control this voice by deciding to listen to neutral or positive voices only. Neutral voices tell us that things are not good or bad (for example, "Everyone gets angry"). Positive ones tell us things are good ("Anger can keep us safe").

What are some other things a neutral voice could say about anger?

_____

_____

_____

_____

_____

_____

_____

_____

What are some other things a positive voice could say about anger?

_____

_____

_____

_____

_____

_____

_____

_____

_____

_____

_____

_____

_____

_____

_____

_____

_____

How am I feeling right now?

I feel this way because _____

_____

Managing anger means that we are able to deal with it in positive ways. This can be hard at first. Think about a time when you managed anger in a positive way. Draw what happened.

MY MANTRAS

How am I feeling right now?

I feel this way because _____

_____

Positive mantras are repeated statements that help us think differently about something. It should be simple like, "I am safe," or "I am in control." Write a few statements you could tell yourself when you are upset.

_____

_____

_____

_____

_____

_____

_____

Practice saying these statements in your head over and over.

Do you like saying mantras to yourself?

TALKING TO MYSELF

How am I feeling right now?

I feel this way because _____

_____

Positive self-talk is a way to train our inside voice. Think about a time when you were angry. Fill in the following statements with neutral or positive words.

I was angry, but I handled it well because

_____

_____

Even though I was angry, I was able to

_____

_____

I do a better job at handling my anger when I

_____

_____

How am I feeling right now?

I feel this way because _____

_____

Think about something that makes you angry. Draw it happening. Now, add some thought bubbles with positive thoughts.

POSITIVE THOUGHTS

How am I feeling right now?

I feel this way because _____

_____

We can change our thoughts to help us manage anger. When we think of anger in a positive way, it can help us be calm. Think about a time when you were angry.

What thoughts did you have?

_____

_____

_____

_____

_____

_____

_____

_____

_____

_____

What thoughts would be more positive?

_____

_____

_____

_____

_____

_____

_____

How could those positive thoughts have helped you feel better?

_____

_____

_____

_____

_____

_____

_____

_____

LET IT GO

How am I feeling right now?

I feel this way because _____

_____

We can let go of negative thoughts about anger. This can help us feel better.

Write about a time you were able to let go of angry thoughts.

_____

_____

_____

_____

_____

How did it feel to let go of the negative thoughts?

_____

_____

_____

_____

How am I feeling right now?

I feel this way because _____

_____

Feelings talk to us through our thoughts. Think about a few different feelings. Write what you think when you feel that way.

When I feel _____ *, I think* _____

_____

_____

_____

When I feel _____ *, I think* _____

_____

_____

_____

When I feel _____ *, I think* _____

_____

_____

How am I feeling right now?

I feel this way because _____

_____

We can think about lots of ways that feelings help us. For example, feelings can help us understand what is going on around us. Think about a time when you were upset.

What were your feelings?

_____

_____

How were those feelings helpful or hurtful?

_____

_____

How could your thoughts have allowed your feelings to be more helpful?

_____

_____

How am I feeling right now?

I feel this way because _____

_____

Feelings keep us safe. They protect us from other feelings that make us feel vulnerable. For example, if we are scared to do something, we might feel angry instead of afraid. Think about a time when you were upset.

What feeling were you trying to protect yourself from?

_____

_____

_____

_____

How could you rewrite your thoughts so you still felt safe?

_____

_____

_____

_____

_____

How am I feeling right now?

I feel this way because _____

_____

Our thoughts can have two sides. The negative side tells us that we are right to be angry and hurt others. The positive side tells us that we can handle anger calmly. Think about a time when you were angry. Draw your thoughts for both the negative and positive sides.

How am I feeling right now?

I feel this way because _____

_____

How we think often becomes who we are. If we *think* about anger a lot we will *be* angry a lot. Thinking about ourselves in positive ways can also help manage anger.

Write 10 qualities about yourself.

_____

_____

_____

_____

_____

What is one quality you like the most about yourself? Why?

_____

_____

_____

_____

How am I feeling right now?

I feel this way because _____

_____

We can use creativity to help us understand anger. This can be done through art or imagination, whether we think we're good artists or not. Creativity is limitless.

Describe the kind of art you like to create.

_____

_____

_____

_____

_____

_____

_____

_____

_____

_____

_____

What materials do you like to use?

_____

_____

_____

_____

_____

_____

_____

_____

How do you like to share or show your art?

_____

_____

_____

_____

_____

_____

_____

_____

_____

BUBBLE POP

How am I feeling right now?

I feel this way because _____

_____

We can calm our thoughts by imagining them as bubbles and learning to pop the negative thoughts. Practice by following these steps.

1. Find a quiet place to sit or lie down.

2. Let your mind wander.

3. When your mind drifts to negative thoughts, imagine yourself quickly popping the thought.

4. When your mind finds positive thoughts, imagine the thought bubble getting bigger and bigger.

Did you like this exercise?

How am I feeling right now?

I feel this way because _____

_____

Drawing can be a great way to express yourself. Use this space to express yourself by drawing anything you like. Use different materials and colors to showcase your creative self.

STOP AND REWIND

How am I feeling right now?

I feel this way because _____

_____

Our imaginations are unlimited. We can even rewind and redo an upsetting situation to prepare us for the next time we're upset.

Describe a situation that was upsetting.

_____

_____

_____

_____

How would you rewind and redo that situation to make it better?

_____

_____

_____

_____

How am I feeling right now?

I feel this way because _____

_____

It can help us be less angry if we look at a situation through a different lens. This means seeing a situation from someone else's perspective. Think about an upsetting situation you had recently.

What was upsetting to you?

_____

_____

_____

_____

_____

How might someone else see or think about it?

_____

_____

_____

_____

SING IT LOUD

I feel this way because _____

_____

Singing can be a great way to creatively manage anger. We can sing along to music or even make up our own songs!

Write a short song you could sing when you are upset.

_____

_____

_____

_____

_____

_____

_____

_____

_____

_____

How am I feeling right now?

I feel this way because _____

_____

Laughter is one of the best ways to manage anger. Watching funny videos or making up jokes can help a lot.

Write a few jokes you could tell when you are upset.

_____

_____

_____

_____

_____

_____

_____

_____

_____

_____

How am I feeling right now?

I feel this way because _____

_____

Water has a natural calming effect. Playing with water can help us manage anger. For example, pouring water into different cups or splashing water in a sink can be relaxing.

What type of water play would be relaxing for you?

_____

_____

_____

_____

_____

How could you do this when you are upset?

_____

_____

_____

_____

How am I feeling right now?

I feel this way because _____

_____

Dancing can lift our spirits in many ways. It is hard to dance and not smile. Try the following steps the next time you are upset.

1. Go to a place where you can be alone.

2. Play some music or think of a tune in your head.

3. Move your body to the tune.

How did that feel?

_____

_____

_____

_____

_____

_____

_____

KINDNESS COUNTS

How am I feeling right now?

I feel this way because _____

_____

Kindness is the opposite of anger. It is a great way to deal with things that are upsetting. Just thinking about kind things can make a big difference.

Describe a kind thing that has happened to you lately.

_____

_____

_____

_____

_____

_____

_____

_____

_____

_____

How did it make you feel?

_____

_____

_____

_____

_____

_____

_____

How could you do kind things for others?

_____

_____

_____

_____

_____

_____

_____

_____

KINDNESS SHIELD

How am I feeling right now?

I feel this way because _____

_____

Kindness can shield us from upsetting feelings. Think about four things that other people do for you that you really like. Draw them here.

How am I feeling right now?

I feel this way because _____

_____

Doing kind things for others can make us feel better. It can be the best medicine when we're grumpy or upset. The next time you are upset, try it.

1. Think of someone you can do something for.

2. Think about what they might like.

3. Do it for them.

4. Don't expect anything from them in return.

How did it feel doing something for someone?

_____

_____

_____

_____

_____

_____

COMPLIMENTS

I feel this way because _____

_____

Compliments are nice things you say to others. Saying nice things to others is kind. Think of three people you know. Fill in the statements with compliments for them.

I like your _____

You are _____

You have a nice _____

Write a few more compliments of your own.

_____

_____

_____

_____

_____

_____

How am I feeling right now?

I feel this way because _____

_____

Gratitude is when we are thankful. When we are upset, we often only think about negative things. Remembering why we are thankful can help us process anger.

What are some things you are thankful for?

_____

_____

_____

_____

How can you remember these things the next time you are upset?

_____

_____

_____

_____

SAYING THANKS

How am I feeling right now?

I feel this way because _____

_____

We can let others know how their kindness makes us feel. Do this the next time someone does something nice for you.

1. Accept the nice act or gift.

2. Look at the person.

3. Say thank you.

4. Tell them how their kindness made you feel.

How did saying thanks feel? Write three words to describe how you felt after this exercise.

_____

_____

_____

_____

_____

_____

How am I feeling right now?

I feel this way because _____

_____

Helping others makes us feel good. It allows us a chance to do something nice for someone.

Who could you help?

_____

_____

What could you do that would be helpful?

_____

_____

How do you think they would feel?

_____

_____

FORGIVENESS

How am I feeling right now?

I feel this way because _____

_____

Holding grudges, or not forgiving someone, keeps anger alive.
Forgiving others can make us feel much better.

What is something you hold a grudge about?

_____

_____

_____

_____

How can you release this grudge?

_____

_____

_____

_____

_____

How am I feeling right now?

I feel this way because _____

_____

Love is another feeling that is the opposite of anger. Love is one of the best cures when we're upset.

List all the people you love.

_____

_____

What do you love the most about them?

_____

_____

How is your life better with them in it?

_____

_____

CREATING LOVE

I feel this way because _____

_____

When we create things for others, it expresses love. It is a way to share your talents with people. For example, you might be great at writing stories or building with blocks.

1. Think of something you like to do or make.

2. Gather all your supplies.

3. Create something unique.

4. Share it with a friend.

How did it feel to create something and give it to someone?

_____

_____

_____

_____

_____

_____

_____

How am I feeling right now?

I feel this way because _____

_____

We have done a lot of thinking about anger. Take this chance to draw a new version of you. Draw some of the tools or thoughts you have learned.

About the Author

 Hiedi France, EdD, the mother of two wonderful teenagers, is a school psychologist who has devoted her career to helping children succeed. She earned a BS in psychology at Northern Illinois University, a MEd in school psychology at Loyola University, and an EdD in educational leadership (focusing on social justice) from Lewis University. Dr. France has worked with students with mental health needs in the education system since 2001. She applies her studies of education and psychology to support the social-emotional and psychological needs of students. Her passion is for all students to succeed and be the best versions of themselves. She has written two books: *Mindfulness for Little Ones* and *The Empathy Workbook for Kids*. These books have been in all major markets and were even highlighted in the mental health section of Target. Dr. France is also the founder of Behavior Savers, which makes easy-to-use social-emotional resources for educators.

CPSIA information can be obtained
at www.ICGtesting.com
Printed in the USA
JSHW030321041121
20120JS00003B/3